JUPITER

MURRAY "OAK" TAPETA

NORWOOD HOUSE PRESS

Cataloging-in-Publication Data

Names: Tapeta, Murray.
Title: Jupiter / Murray Tapeta.
Description: Buffalo, NY : Norwood House Press, 2026. | Series: Outer space | Includes glossary and index.
Identifiers: ISBN 9781978574809 (pbk.) | ISBN 9781978574816 (library bound) | ISBN 9781978574823 (ebook)
Subjects: LCSH: Jupiter (Planet)--Juvenile literature.
Classification: LCC QB661.T374 2026 | DDC 523.45--dc23

Published in 2026 by
Norwood House Press
2544 Clinton Street
Buffalo, NY 14224

Copyright © 2026 Norwood House Press
Designer: Rhea Magaro
Editor: Kim Thompson

Photo credits: Cover, p. 1, 5, 9, 15, 21 NASA Images; p. 6, 7 Vadim Sadovski/Shutterstock.com; p. 8 Dima Moroz/Shutterstock.com; pp. 10, 12, 13, 18 Artsiom P/Shutterstock.com; p. 11 Vladi333/Shutterstock.com; p. 16 Cinefootage Visuals; p. 17 Andreas Liem/Shutterstock.com;

All rights reserved. No part of this book may be reproduced in any form without permission in writing from the publisher, except by a reviewer.

Printed in the United States of America

Some of the images in this book illustrate individuals who are models. The depictions do not imply actual situations or events.

CPSIA compliance information: Batch #CSNHP26: For further information contact Norwood House Press at 1-800-237-9932.

TABLE OF CONTENTS

Where Is Jupiter? 4

How Was Jupiter Discovered? 8

What Is It Like on Jupiter? 10

Has Jupiter Been Explored? 19

Glossary 22

Thinking Questions 23

Index 24

About the Author 24

Where Is Jupiter?

Our **solar system** has eight planets. Jupiter is the fifth planet from the Sun. It is the largest planet by far! About 1,000 Earths could fit inside Jupiter.

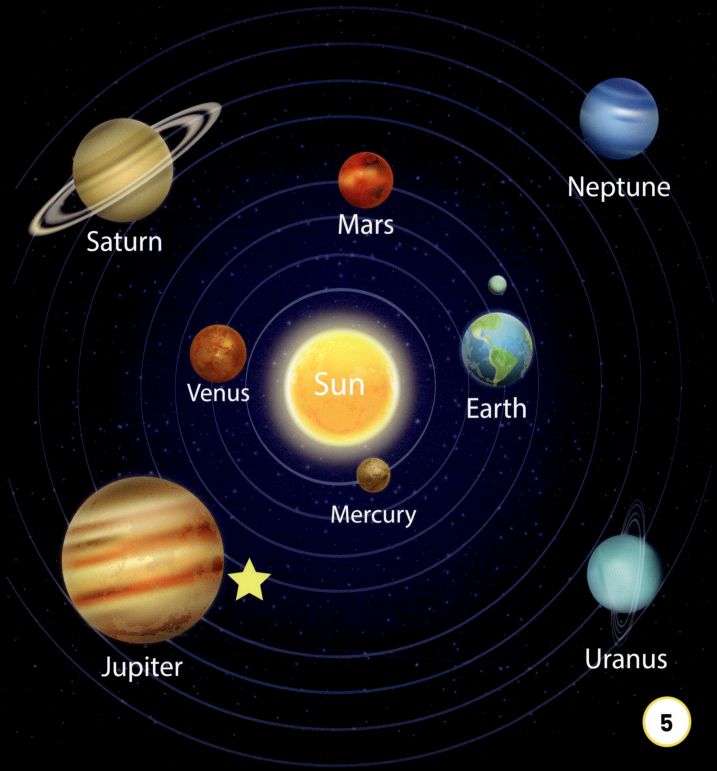

Jupiter is about 484 million miles (778 million kilometers) from the Sun. Getting to Jupiter from Earth would take nearly a year.

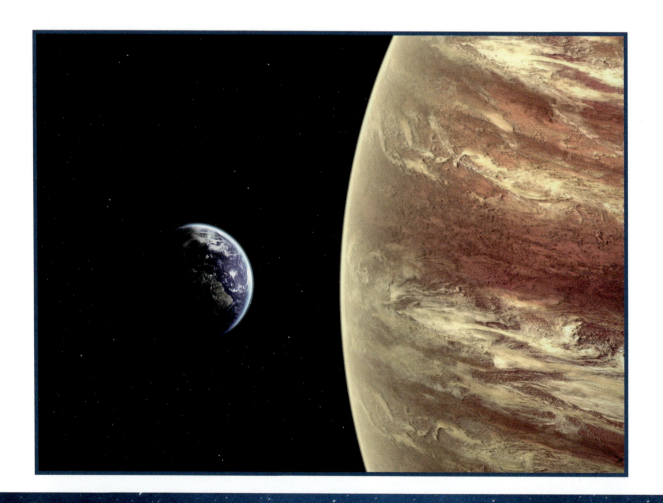

One year on Jupiter lasts 4,333 Earth days. That is about 12 Earth years. It takes Jupiter that long to **orbit** the Sun.

How Was Jupiter Discovered?

Ancient people noticed Jupiter when they looked up at the night sky. It looked like a big, bright, yellow star. They named the planet Jupiter after the king of the Roman gods.

Italian **astronomer** Galileo Galilei first saw Jupiter through a **telescope** in 1610.

What Is It Like on Jupiter?

You could not stand on Jupiter. It does not have a solid surface. The planet is made mostly of the gases **hydrogen** and **helium**. It is called "the gas giant."

It is freezing cold on Jupiter. The thick **atmosphere** is full of swirling clouds. They create colorful stripes and spots.

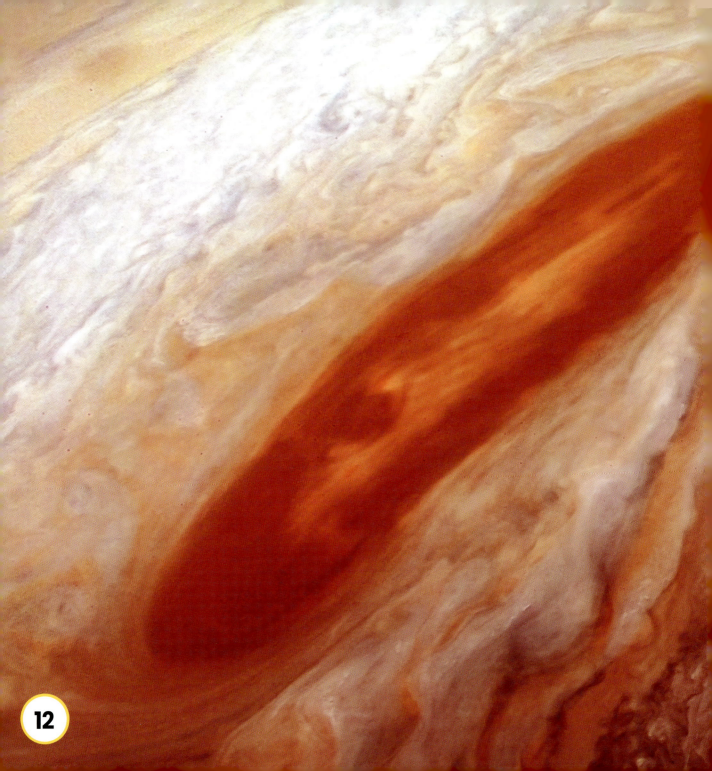

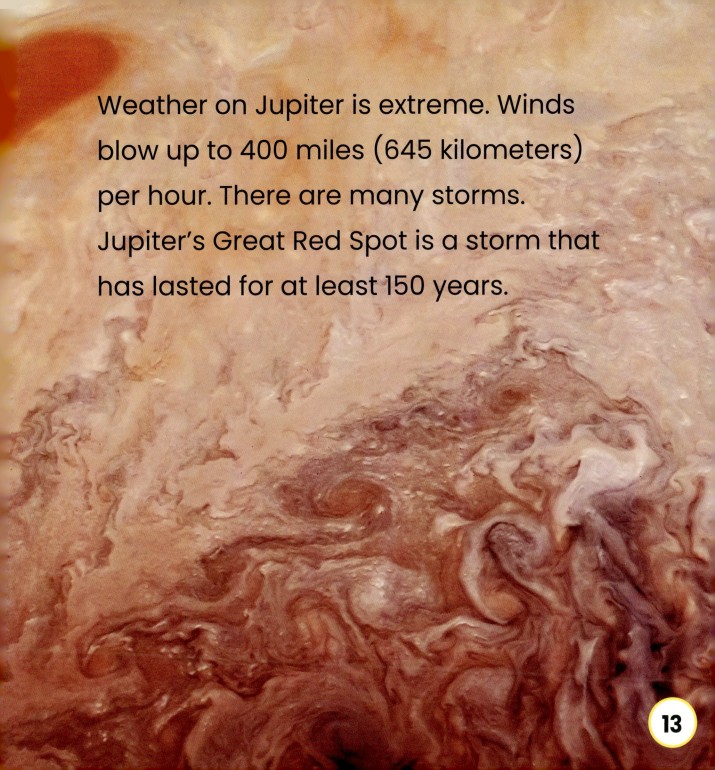

Weather on Jupiter is extreme. Winds blow up to 400 miles (645 kilometers) per hour. There are many storms. Jupiter's Great Red Spot is a storm that has lasted for at least 150 years.

At least 90 moons orbit Jupiter. Ganymede is the solar system's largest moon. Io is covered in volcanoes. Scientists think there may be water on Callisto and Europa.

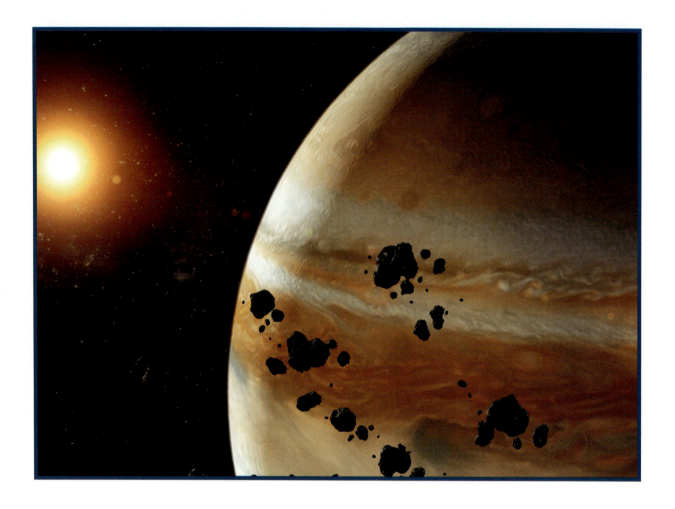

Gravity on Jupiter is much stronger than it is on Earth. It is strong enough to pull **asteroids** toward the planet.

Scientists think Jupiter formed nearly five billion years ago. Gravity pulled together swirling dust and gas. Over time, the giant planet formed.

Has Jupiter Been Explored?

Jupiter is made of gas, so nothing can land there. **Satellites** have been sent to fly close to the planet for over 50 years. They have sent photos and data back to Earth.

The spacecraft *Europa Clipper* will reach Jupiter's moon Europa in 2030. It will help scientists understand if living things could survive there.

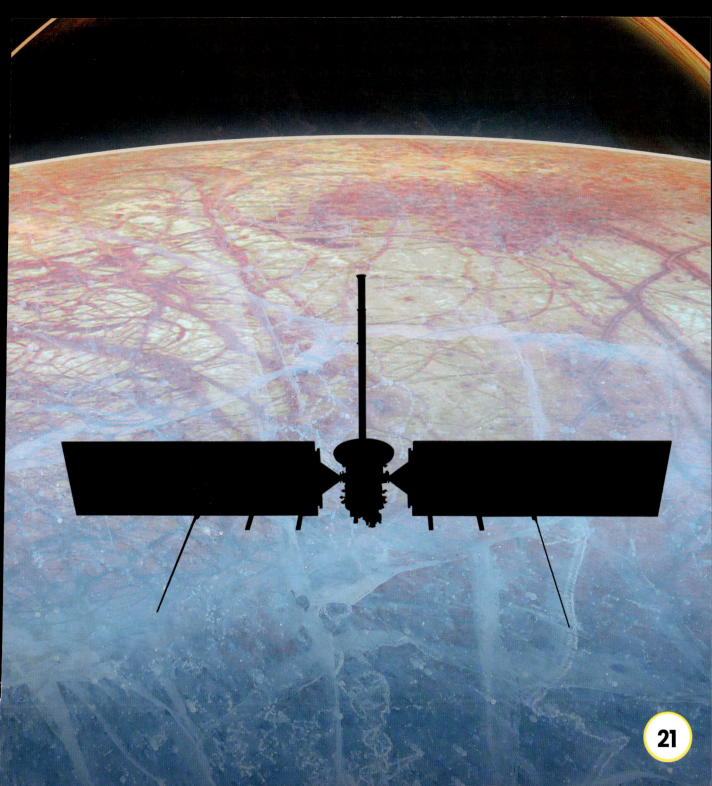

Glossary

asteroids (AS-tuh-roids): small, rocky objects that orbit a planet or the Sun; objects in space made from leftover material from when the solar system was formed

astronomer (uh-STRAH-nuh-mer): a scientist who studies objects in the sky, including planets, galaxies, and stars

atmosphere (AT-muhs-feer): the mixture of gases that surrounds a planet; air

gravity (GRAV-i-tee): an invisible force that pulls objects toward each other and keeps them from floating away

helium (HEE-lee-uhm): a light, colorless gas that does not burn

hydrogen (HYE-druh-juhn): a gas with no smell or color that is lighter than air and that easily catches fire

orbit (OR-bit): to follow a curved path around a larger body in space

satellites (SAT-uh-lites): spacecrafts sent into orbit around a planet, moon, or other object in space

solar system (SOH-lur SIS-tuhm): the Sun and everything that orbits around it

telescope (TEL-uh-skope): an instrument that helps people see distant objects

Thinking Questions

1. Where did the planet Jupiter get its name?

2. Describe the weather on Jupiter.

3. Name two of Jupiter's moons.

4. What does Jupiter look like in Earth's night sky?

5. How do satellites help scientists study Jupiter?

Index

atmosphere 11

Earth 4, 6, 7, 16, 19

Europa Clipper 20

Galilei, Galileo 9

Ganymede 14, 15

gravity 16, 17

Great Red Spot 13

moons 14, 15, 20

orbit 7, 14

Sun 4, 6, 7

About the Author

Murray "Oak" Tapeta was born in a cabin without plumbing in Montana. Growing up in the great outdoors, he became a lover of nature. He earned the nickname "Oak" after climbing to the top of an oak tree at the age of three. Oak loves to read and write. He has written many books about events in history and other subjects that fascinate him. He prefers spending time in the wilderness with his dog Birchy.